C000078876

HOW TO BE A...

CHAPETTE

HOW TO BE A… CHAPETTE

Summersdale Publishers Ltd
46 West Street
Chichester
West Sussex
PO19 1RP
UK

www.summersdale.com

Printed and bound in China

ISBN: 978-1-84953-588-5

Substantial discounts on bulk quantities of Summersdale books are available to corporations, professional associations and other organisations. For details contact Nicky Douglas by telephone: +44 (0) 1243 756902, fax: +44 (0) 1243 786300 or email: nicky@summersdale.com.

HOW TO BE A...

CHAPETTE

A Nifty Guide for First-Rate Ladies

Illustrations by
Adam Nickel

Daisy Loveday

summersdale

*To all practitioners
in the art of being
a Lady*

CONTENTS

INTRODUCTION

WELCOME, LADIES, to *How to Be a… Chapette*, your nifty pocket guide to all matters relating to the art of vintage styling and classy comportment. This book is intended to offer friendly advice that might help one achieve the look, attitude and general sophistications of that beacon of style and intelligence known as the Lady.

But what is a 'Chapette'? A Chapette is a 'fine sort'; a woman of refined qualities that are reflected in the way she looks and the way she acts; a lady with a considerate yet freethinking attitude and a taste for retro fashions.

Although this book takes its inspiration from the trends and mores of bygone eras – most notably the forties and fifties – these will be used purely as suggestions to be interpreted for the modern day, rather than as reiterations of lamentable attitudes towards what one 'should' and 'shouldn't' do.

In this author's opinion, what truly defines a Chapette is not the desire to acquire a millimetre-perfect up-do or a tastefully-fitted original shirtwaister dress, but rather the desire to act with good form and grace in all situations. A Chapette is masterful enough to show refinement but brave enough to not to be unnecessarily constrained by ceremony; to have the wits to know how to act with class but to have the imagination to not be limited by it.

Above all of the specific assertions made in this book regarding the material refinements of a Chapette, one thought should remain within the reader's mind:

A Chapette is, in essence…

Charming
Honest
Attentive
Presentable
Every
Time
To
Everyone

With that idea firmly in mind, let's get to it!

CHAPETTE

The Look

THE MARK of a true Chapette is in her heart rather than her hairband, granted – but, like the swan, she is most readily identified by her elegant silhouette: the sweep of her victory rolls; the playful flutter of her neckerchief and the flattering cut of her A-line dress. These things, along with other quirky yet classic adornments, constitute the image of the Chapette.

A golden rule to keep in mind: if you're aiming for a full-on vintage get-up rather than a modern twist – be it preppy shirt-and-skirt casual or cocktail-dress chic – be sure to execute the look coherently and consistently, with *every* item in keeping with the style you're aiming to achieve.

COIFFURE

HAIRSTYLES EXPRESS just as much about character as any other facet of the Chapette look, especially since one can shape the hair so variously. That said, the aspiring Lady may refer to many so-called 'classic' styles to achieve a look that is suitably chic. When choosing, consider that a hairstyle should suit the shape of one's face: for those ladies with a more heart-shaped face, an upright style, such as a bouffant, will complement nicely, whereas those ladies with an oval visage can look great with a flatter, perhaps side-swept style.

Whichever you choose, some kind of hairspray or pomade and pins will no doubt be involved, so make sure you have plenty to hand!

Classic Retro Hairstyles

The Half-Up, Half-Down

This style is good for day or night and is quintessentially vintage, most often seen with victory rolls at the front and the hair natural or wavy at the back. To form your rolls, start with a centre parting and roll the sides and top of your hair back and pin. Some backcombing may be required before rolling commences to give thinner hair the volume to complete the look. Waves are an especially nice touch for the back.

Side-Swept Waves

Glossy, sumptuous waves, à la Veronica Lake, ooze glamour and sophistication and are ideal for a classy evening out. To style, make a side parting and pin up the heavier side. Begin curling (an iron with a 1-inch barrel is best) above your ear on the opposite side to which your parting falls and work your way back. Once this is done, unpin the previously pinned side and repeat the curling process. Once you've finished curling, fix with hairspray and then comb through to caress your curls into tumbling waves.

The Up-Do

There are many retro up-dos to choose from, but the Hepburn bun is neat and chic. A basic bun is straightforward, presuming you have shoulder-length hair (or longer). Brush your hair back into a high ponytail. Backcomb the underside of your ponytail to create volume, but ensure the top is smooth. Wrap your hair around the base of the tail, smooth side out, and pin in place. Use hairspray to hold the bun – you may want to give it a little extra vintage flair by adding a ribbon.

Chapette Fact

Marcel Grateau (1852–1936) is believed to have acquired the first patent on curling irons back in 1905 in the US and is responsible for the technique known as 'marcelling'.

STYLISH ATTIRE is an area in which the refinements of the Chapette are allowed to unfurl like the petals of a sweet-smelling corsage. Clothes don't make a woman, but they speak volumes about her character; for the Chapette, the message that comes from her attire should suggest confidence and flair.

There are many time-honoured styles for the aspiring Chapette to seize upon, but perhaps what really distinguishes a lady from the run-of-the-mill retro rookie is attention to detail: authenticity in fabric, colour and cut will make the difference when selecting clothing (as opposed to a modern 'reworking'). However, this can be pricey, so if you're opting for the High Street all it takes is a little careful consideration when selecting your clothes. Perhaps the best way to achieve a coherent look is to search for images from the era you're after – that way you can see what works with what before you go ahead and break out your purse!

Skirts, Stockings and Other Particulars

A selection of nifty retro skirts is a staple in the Chapette wardrobe. Vintage styles are generally patterned (often floral) and/or pleated, and often with an generous cut, which means they can be coupled with a relatively plain top and you still have a dandy look without too much effort. Underwear, including stockings, is one area in which you can go to town with exquisite reproduction girdles, garters and corsets for a glamorous (and expensive!) look, or simply settle for comfort with some of your own favourites.

Blouses and Trousers

Chapette style isn't all about flowers and frills - simplicity is a key part of the look, and nothing says simple elegance like a pair of fifties pedal-pushers or capri pants with a snappy, fitted shirt. Picture Audrey or Marilyn and you'll get the idea. Forties-era swing pants, coupled with a slim-fitting blouse or short-sleeved top, can add a little more attitude to the outfit.

Cardigans

Not just for grandmas and librarians, oh no! Cardigans are cute and comfortable. They can be worn with all of the previous outfits, including dresses. If your dress is patterned, you may want to keep your cardi simple, though that doesn't mean they will be lacking in style: many vintage cardis have a distinctive button-to-neck design and are cut to flatter – and remember, real wool (especially cashmere!) has more character than your run-of-the-mill synthetic material. For a more casual yet classy way to sport your cardigan, why not try wearing it over-the-shoulder, holding it in place with a nice vintage brooch.

Dresses and Overcoats

Nothing is prettier than a Chapette in a sweet-looking shirtwaister dress, but this is just the tip of the iceberg in terms of vintage styles. Tea dresses look classy and charming, while wiggle dresses are flirty and figure-hugging. As long as you work within the parameters of 'vintage' and keep your style consistent, you'll look the part.

Vintage coats are often as stylish as dresses – a forties-inspired double-breasted trench coat with a cinched waist is chic, while a fifties-look swing coat is more on the cute side. Of course, you could opt for the opulence of fake fur if you want something a bit more glamorous!

Shoes

Again, there is a world of style to explore with vintage shoes. One staple is the Mary Jane shoe, which tends to suit many retro outfits, but consider the ballerina pump when sporting a more practical get-up or the stiletto heel for a femme fatale feel. Don't be afraid of more chunky, square 'Chappish' styles – they're Chapette too!

Chapette Fact

The stiletto heel first achieved popularity in the mid-fifties, with designers such as Roger Vivier at the forefront. The word is derived from the Italian *stiletto*, which means 'small, thin blade'.

'Dress shabbily and they remember the dress; dress impeccably and they remember the woman.'

Coco Chanel

ACCESSORIES ARE the finishing touches to the look which separate the natty from the newbie. A girl in a retro dress is just that, whereas a girl in a retro dress with a pair of elegant gloves, a delicately placed tilt hat and a set of antique pearls is one swanky dame. Again, the rule of consistency applies: a bright pink Hello Kitty umbrella will do nothing but clash horribly with your vintage enamel brooch, therefore, when choosing your accessories, aim for items that are in keeping with the vintage style of your outfit. Aside from being extra style details in your ensemble, most accessories have a practical purpose, so don't be daunted by the notion that you're being overly fancy with your hat or your silk scarf.

Bows and Belts

 These two items are all but essential to the Chapette ensemble and are quick and easy accent pieces that will add a dash of colour and class to your outfit. A shirtwaister dress is practically incomplete without a belt of some description, whether it be one that blends with the dress fabric itself or one that creates a nice contrast. Hand-tied hair bows can be small and subtle off to the side or, if you're inventive with your head scarf, big and bold, acting as a hairband and sitting prettily on the top of your head. Both are the perfect way to add some individuality to your outfit.

Boleros and Shawls

Boleros are quintessentially Chapette and can make for a simple but impressive addition to an outfit. They can be sassy (collared and fitted for an evening dress) or sweet (knitted for a more practical look), depending on the overall tone of your ensemble. Big sister to the bolero is the shawl – the size and shape of these items can sometimes detract from the stylishness of your outfit, however if you opt for a smaller, more delicate lacy number, you will not weigh yourself or your look down. The stole is another glamorous vintage staple.

Gloves, Hats and Scarves

Wearing short gloves, which end at the wrist, with a day dress is an easy way to look vintage. Longer gloves tend to suit a sleeveless dress (or one that shows more of your arms). In all cases, they should match your bag, shoes or hat. The choice of hats for the aspiring Chapette is vast: pillbox hats are showy and formal; large brim hats are classy; berets are chic; while a trilby is practical and snappy. A retro standard is to wear your hat at a slight angle. Scarf squares are a delightful way of dressing up a mac, especially if you opt for a lightweight patterned affair and wear it in the timeless around-the-head fashion.

Jewellery

Pearls are a no-brainer for any retro occasion. Bangles, bracelets and brooches are less obvious but original examples of all of these can be found with a little research – and chances are they will not break the bank, especially if you're not looking to imitate Audrey's sparkling diamonds too closely! Coloured bead and rhinestone necklaces are very fifties, as are pearl collars and dress clips.

Chapette Fact

'Tiffany blue', associated with the jewellery company's packaging, is actually protected by trademark – the Pantone colour code is 1837.

'VINTAGE' MAKE-UP – that is, cosmetic styles inspired by the forties and fifties – can vary quite a bit. Make-up is also very personal and you may not want to make stark changes in this area for the sake of a certain look. However, keeping in line with the 'chic but practical' Chapette motto, this author would be inclined to suggest that less is more; little hints and touches here and there are best. If you're not a make-up person, or if you feel confident enough to show the world your real face, you won't look out of place going 'naked'. Arguably the most striking feature of vintage make-up is red lips – think of Rita Hayworth, Lucille Ball, Doris Day, Ava Gardner and, of course, Marilyn. In contrast to the striking lips, the majority of make-up colours of the time were light pastels. This is reflected in the dresses of the era, so if you're going for co-ordination, keep this in mind.

Face

A smooth, even complexion is the soft, clean canvas upon which many women of the fifties painted their look, often referred to in a somewhat unflattering way as the 'mask effect'. A generous layer of matt foundation can be enhanced with a touch of peach- (if your lipstick is of a warmer red tone) or rose-coloured powder (if your lipstick is a cooler, pink tone) applied to the apple of the cheek.

Eyes

Simple yet striking eye make-up is the way to capture the vintage look. Eyeshadow of pastel colour can be applied lightly, whereas mascara can be used generously. Eyeliner is the key here, however. To achieve the oh-so-sexy 'winged' line, follow these steps:

1. Start at the middle of your upper lid and create a strong line which covers the arch of your lid, but not into the corner of your eye. Draw this as close to your eyelash possible.

2. Draw a finer line towards the line you just applied, starting from the corner of your eye.

3. Add the all-important 'wing' by starting from your last lash outwards and drawing an upwardly curved line.

4. Next, draw a line from the end of your wing back to your upper-lid line to create an empty triangle.

5. Fill in the triangle with your pencil. *Mee-ow!*

Lips

The main event in the fifties make-up arena was the lips – voluptuous, kissable, vivid. Deep pinks and intense reds are the way to go to achieve this, not forgetting the lipliner to make your mouth appear fuller and more luscious. As a simple guide for lipstick colours: orangey-red lipsticks match well with blonde hair, as well as red hair and other medium-dark colours; burgundy-red lipsticks look wonderful with dark hair.

Chapette Fact

The first kiss-proof lipstick was introduced by American chemist Hazel Bishop in 1950 – it was called 'No-Smear Lipstick' and it was so popular that her sales increased from around $50,000 in 1950 to over $10 million in 1953.

Make-up Innovations of the Fifties

Max Factor

The introduction of Technicolor film in movies meant there was an increased call for the make-up that gave the stars a glamorous glow. Max Factor's 'panchromatic' make-up – better known as 'Pan Cake' – left a silky sheen on the skin, which did just that.

Estée Lauder

This New York-based company was one of the first brands to introduce the idea of free cosmetic samples for customers – including mini lipsticks, eyeshadows and face creams – which helped open up a world of products to an eager public.

Rimmel

Eugène Rimmel took this London-based family firm to new heights when he opened a flagship store in Regent Street. The fifties saw its sales of eye make-up, mascara in particular, rise significantly.

'Beneath the make-up and behind the smile I am just a girl who wishes for the world.'

Marilyn Monroe

CHAPETTE

The Character

THE CHARMING look of a Chapette is necessarily complemented by an attractive and engaging character. This section presents some typically vintage persuasions in the areas of parlance, music, literature and film, which may be of special interest to the Chapette.

PARLANCE

THE FIFTIES brought with it a new rebellious side in many areas of popular culture. Many writers actually attribute this era to the birth of the teenager as we know it - thinking differently and questioning the established order were new luxuries beginning to be afforded to the post-war teens and it showed in their language, especially in the States. 'Jive talking', largely derived from jazz performer Cab Calloway's lyrics, laid the foundations for the hipster slang that permeated America in this era. Rather than being stereotypically 'ladylike', it was defiant, crude and wildly imaginative. Whilst a careful choice of cultivated words is always encouraged for the aspiring Chapette, the freethinking, creative spirit represented by slang in the fifties is bound to provide inspiration for your own endeavours.

Jive Talking with the Hep Cats

Here are some examples of the weird and wonderful world of fifties slang:

Storked
expecting a baby.

Legit
legitimate.

Know your groceries
'in the know'; being aware.

Canary
a female vocalist.

MANY A famous lady exemplified her wit and wisdom with a quotable phrase or two – here are some of the finest:

'I never say "never" and I never say "always".'
Grace Kelly

❤

'Men are creatures with two legs and eight hands.'
Jayne Mansfield

❤

'There is a fountain of youth: it is your mind, your talents, the creativity you bring to your life.'
Sophia Loren

'Big girls need big diamonds.'
Elizabeth Taylor

❤

'I want to wear beautiful clothes and look pretty. I want to smile and I want to make people laugh. And that's all I want.'
Doris Day

❤

'Anyone who has a continuous smile on his face conceals a toughness that is almost frightening.'
Greta Garbo

❤

'I don't mind living in a man's world as long as I can be a woman in it.'
Marilyn Monroe

THE FIFTIES brought with it one of the most - if not *the* most - significant movements in popular music: rock 'n' roll. It sent guys and gals crazy in equal measure - it was provocative, lively and FUN! If you're dressed head-to-toe in your vintage splendour it's practically criminal not to go out to a club or dancing venue to strut your stuff in style - whether it be in the ballroom or at the record shop.

The Art of Listening

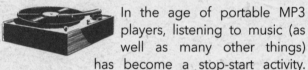

In the age of portable MP3 players, listening to music (as well as many other things) has become a stop-start activity. However, in this Chapette's opinion to truly appreciate the love and craft that has gone into a piece of music one must kick back, relax and become immersed in it. The best way to do this is in comfortable (preferably home) surroundings, with no other distractions. For a truly vintage ambiance vinyl records, rather than MP3s, come into their own. With LPs the whole listening experience is more involved and attention-holding and acquires an air of sophistication. If you're not the kind of person who likes to lose themselves in a record, old-fashioned music to set a romantic mood is always a winner.

Swinging, Shaking and Serenading

Ballroom and Swing

If you're the kind of girl who loves to be graceful and demure, you may want to consider giving ballroom dancing a try. It often requires elegance over exertion, and it's a delightfully formal way to enjoy an evening with your partner – or to acquire one! Of course, it will help if you're familiar with some of the typical styles of music used: if it's a 'traditional' ballroom event you might encounter a waltz or a tango. Check out the more animated but supremely classy swing tunes of the Glenn Miller Orchestra, Benny Goodman or Count Basie if you're after something a bit more lively – great for dancing and for listening!

Rock 'n' Roll

Jumping and jiving to a rock 'n' roll classic is endless fun and can be enjoyed with or without a partner. In the more formal sense it's closely related to swing, but essentially it's all about letting go – twisting and shouting! There are hundreds upon hundreds of rock 'n' roll records to be enjoyed – from Little Richard to The Big Bopper – and the true classics remain as such and are as easy to spot as a ribbon at a rockabilly night.

Vocal Artists

Female vocalists of the vintage era are the epitome of sultriness and soul. If you're looking for inspiration for your heart and mind, listen to tracks by the 'big three' jazz singers – Ella Fitzgerald, Sarah Vaughan and Billie Holiday – or if you're looking for something with a more European feel, check out Vera Lynn or Edith Piaf. All of these women, and many, many more, will get you in the mood for vintage-inspired frocks and frolics.

'Forgive me if I don't have the words. Maybe I can sing it and you'll understand.'

Ella Fitzgerald

Chapette Musicians and Singers

Sister Rosetta Tharpe

She may not have had a polished, glamorous look, but this African-American performer had a vivacious spirit that would make any Chapette swell with pride. Her gospel style was remarkable, as was her stage presence, when she would perform in her Sunday best while clutching a powerful Gibson SG electric guitar (an instrument which is now a hard rock and heavy metal staple!).

Maria Callas

This New York-born Greek soprano is perhaps the most renowned female opera singer of all time. Her performances were the epitome of effortless beauty. Her voice was exemplary but her career was by no means divine – she experienced a number of scandals, including one which led to her acquiring the moniker 'Tigress'.

Judy Garland

Born Frances Ethel Gumm, this shining star of stage and screen started out performing vaudeville with her siblings. When the group decided to call themselves The Garland Sisters, Frances took on the moniker of 'Judy'. She sang remarkably in many musical films, including of course the unforgettable *The Wizard of Oz* and later as Esther Blodgett in *A Star is Born*.

Barbara Lynn

Barbara Lynn was an audacious African-American blues performer who came to prominence in the sixties as 'the Black Elvis'. Not only did she play lead guitar, she also wrote many of her own songs and toured with soul and blues greats, such as Gladys Knight, Al Green and B. B. King. Her song 'Oh Baby (We Got a Good Thing Goin')' was covered by The Rolling Stones in 1965.

A WELL-READ lady is never short on interesting conversation; she knows how to use her imagination and has a world of intriguing places, characters and ideas to draw upon. These are all fine things for a Chapette to have at her disposal. The literary universe may provide inspiration in practically every aspect of life, not least in the art of being a Chapette: consider the charming and charitable Jane Eyre; the wit and tenacity of girl-about-town Sally Jay Gorce in *The Dud Avocado* or the resourceful and determined Flora Poste in *Cold Comfort Farm*.

The Library of Chapette

HOW TO BE A... CHAPETTE

LITTLE WOMEN

The Portrait of a Lady

To Kill a Mockingbird

PROMETHEA

THE LITERARY world is replete with tales of admirable women that may inspire a budding Chapette. Here's a handful:

Little Women by Louisa May Alcott
A classic tale of young girls finding their way as women in a prescriptive society and one of 'non-traditional womanhood'. Democracy – in relationships and in the household – is the redeeming force in the novel, which transforms the fate of many of the female characters and so offers encouragement in the way of self-respect and defying expectations.
Chapette Factor: 7/10 – a classic, empowering period piece. Minus three marks for the fuddy-duddy frills and bonnets.

The Portrait of a Lady by Henry James
This is the story of feisty female Isabel Archer who, despite being strongly independent, finds herself in a marriage gone awry. Isabel's seemingly paradoxical decision to stick it out with her deplorable husband Osmond raises the dilemma of whether it is nobler to accept your fate and live

up to your commitments, however terrible, or to defy conventions and break free – some serious food for thought.

Chapette Factor: 6/10 – James paints a picture that is appalling and provocative, and in doing so he poses as many questions as he purports to answer.

To Kill a Mockingbird by Harper Lee

Quirky, spirited and inquisitive, Scout Finch is an outstanding role model who invites the reader to hark back to their youthful innocence and consider how they might see things in a different, more accepting, light. She is full of a special imagination and bravery that is touching and commendable – an original outsider and proud of it.

Chapette Factor: 9/10 – a kind-hearted, plucky female character with an alternative dress sense – Chapette through and through!

Promethea by Alan Moore

This mystical and mythical comic-book series presents a heroine, Sophie Bangs, as the reincarnation of goddess-like Promethea, the spirit of Imagination. The story is full of magical foes and deathly challenges for Sophie, who ultimately successfully meets her fate and becomes the powerful, exceptional person she is destined to be.

Chapette Factor: 7/10 – a far-out, fantastical foray and a visual feast – a world away from vintage culture, but nonetheless endlessly provocative for free-spirited, freethinking readers.

Chapette Fact

Jo March in *Little Women* was a largely autobiographical character for Louisa May. Unlike the spirited Jo, however, who marries at the end of the novel, Alcott was single throughout her entire life.

THE SILVER screen has been and will perhaps always be wrought with admirable, stylish women. In the early days of cinema, an actor or actress merely appearing on a big screen was enough to cause excitement, but when the glamour of the studio system set in the stars shone brighter than ever. Tales of wild romance and dashing, handsome heroes were abundant - all of which were thoroughly entertaining and thoroughly imitable. Many unforgettable female characters were immortalised in the movies, be it through their memorable outfits, impressive mannerisms or simply for delivering a monumental line.

Classic Chapettes of the Silver Screen

Audrey Hepburn

Audrey is the archetypal Chapette, the very essence of class, charisma and confidence. Her presence on screen was enchanting and unforgettable. Whether it be in the iconic *Breakfast at Tiffany's* or the charming, Oscar-winning *Roman Holiday*, she shines and sets a standard the likes of which many have aspired to. Hepburn was the first actress to win an Oscar, a Golden Globe and a BAFTA Award for a single performance *(Roman Holiday)*.

Chapette Weapon of Choice: the perfect up-do

Katharine Hepburn

Audrey's namesake was of course no relation, but nonetheless Connecticut-born Katharine was a remarkable actress and an intriguing personality. She made her biggest impact in the thirties with roles including Eva Lovelace *(Morning Glory)* and Jo March *(Little Women)*. She was unconventional in her manner and dress sense – a true individual – and despite some career ups and downs she was in movies for more than 60 years.

Chapette Weapon of Choice: killer swing pants

Ginger Rogers

Ginger was born Virginia Katherine McMath and was perhaps best known for being dance partner to the equally gifted Fred Astaire. She won an Oscar for her role in *Kitty Foyle*, in which she also managed to establish a trademark outfit: the Kitty Foyle dress, which, as it came to be known, was a shirtwaister with contrasting collar, buttons and cuffs. Bob Thaves said of Rogers, 'She did everything Fred Astaire did, but she did it backwards and in high heels!'

Chapette Weapon of Choice: the shirtwaister

Ingrid Bergman

Sweet Swedish actress Ingrid Bergman impressed herself on many cinema-goers' hearts with her remarkable performance in *Casablanca*, opposite Humphrey Bogart. Rated in the top five female stars of all time by the AFI (American Film Institute), Bergman worked with Hitchcock in the forties and starred in movies in Italy in later life. She acted in no less than five languages and won three Academy awards.

Chapette Weapon of Choice: a subtle yet sultry visage

'I believe in dressing for the occasion. There's a time for sweater, sneakers and Levis and a time for the full-dress jazz.'

Ginger Rogers

CHAPETTE

In Practice

YOU MAY have perfected styling your retro do, found the ideal vintage get-up, gathered a host of killer accessories and absorbed all the Chapette inspiration your library has to offer; but all of this is worth little unless you can follow it through with a charming and cheerful manner. Any dolled-up Daisy can look the part, but it takes a real lady to exude class and add some extra special touches to those seemingly humdrum everyday exercises.

TO SOME, 'etiquette' is a dirty word. This is somewhat understandable, as it has connotations of unnecessary rules devised by some overinflated, pompous know-it-all back in the days when society was so uptight that one could barely blink without the proper say-so. However, at the heart of etiquette is a simple, shared politeness to one's fellow man and woman, with a bit of added flair to make things seem more special. There is something deeply satisfying in partaking in formal social rituals, perhaps because it acts as a reminder that we are caring, considerate beings – those who can freely enjoy cocktail parties, dinner dances and fine Champagne!

Greetings

Everyone loves to be greeted with a smile and a polite 'hello' or 'how do you do?'. This is less Chapette and more common courtesy, but you'd be surprised at what a difference it can make! If you've been invited to a party, greeting the host might involve presenting them with a small token of gratitude - a bottle of wine, some freshly baked muffins or some other thoughtful gift, depending on what kind of party it is.

At the Table

Manners when dining are appropriate for all occasions and for all people. First and foremost, get your napkin ready by placing it in your lap. If you're desperate to get your hands on those stuffed vine leaves that are just out of arm's reach, don't lean over and grab them, ask somebody to pass them to you. It's common courtesy to serve others before yourself if there's wine and water on the table. When you've finished eating, place your napkin next to, rather than on, your plate. Refrain from applying make-up at the table.

Chapette Fact

The term 'napkin' derives from the French *nappe* (a tablecloth) and *kin*, denoting the 'mini' size. They were used as early as Roman times.

The Art of Conversation

You may feel you've already got the gift of the gab, but the art of polite conversation at any sort of formal gathering is one that may need to be practised. Here are a few golden rules:

Listen – the best compliment you can pay a friend or a new acquaintance is to listen and be attentive when they are speaking and show interest in what they're discussing.

Avoid potentially controversial subjects – discussing sex, politics, money or religion is a sure way to put your foot in it unnecessarily! These subjects have their place among close friends, but when at a polite gathering it's best to avoid them, especially if alcohol is involved.

Mingle – if you have the chance to circulate, make the effort to speak to others, rather than stay talking to your friends or one particular person. This is especially important at a small gathering as it means nobody will feel left out – and you get to speak to even more interesting people!

Thank Yous

If one of your friends or an acquaintance has made a special effort to throw a party or gathering you have attended, the classiest of thank yous is to send them a little handwritten note saying how much you enjoyed and appreciated it. A phone call is just as effective, although it doesn't give you the opportunity to get out that oh-so-cute stationery set you've been meaning to put to use.

THERE ARE, of course, no rules for relaxation – whatever works best for you is what you should stick to, however there are some distinctly Chapette pastimes, which any aspiring all-rounder might want to consider. Being active and constructive with one's spare time is truly commendable and, if nothing else, fun! You needn't force yourself to become a master cupcake-maker or champion ballroom dancer – giving things a go is half the enjoyment. Taking up a hobby, such as baking, crafting or something outdoorsy, gives you the opportunity to meet other likeminded people in a club – or perhaps you could start your own!

Crafting

Crafting is a delightful way to spend an evening or weekend - it's creative and relaxing at the same time. It might involve such thoroughly vintage pursuits as knitting (teacosies are especially quirky and fabulous), crocheting (consider a retro throw for a sofa), or sewing (ideal for customising and repairing clothes). The best thing about crafts like these is that what you're making often has a practical purpose - your crafts can also be gifts for your loved ones.

Baking

Being a fan of the wonder that is cake is one thing, but baking your own is so much more rewarding! Whether you're making Crispy cakes or going full on with a multi-layered sponge with home-made icing, making sweet treats for yourself or for friends and family is a joy and, some may find, relaxing.

Bargain-hunting

A Chapette not only takes pride in her personal appearance but also in her home. A great way to save money and add a personal touch to your decor is to go bargain-hunting at car boot sales for vintage-style furniture to makeover. Even better, search online for a vintage boot fair – you could even dress up to attend.

Picnicking

It sounds simple, but preparing and organising a picnic (weather-permitting of course) is a delight. There's delicious food, wine (or Champagne if you're pushing the boat out), the great outdoors and cute checked blankets! Picnics also afford the opportunity to break out your thoroughly retro picnic basket, complete with old-fashioned dinnerware.

WHAT IS life without celebration? Everyone – Chapette or no – needs time to be footloose and fancy-free. However, reckless abandon should not be in a lady's behavioural vocabulary. There is classy celebration and outright indulgence, and the latter is to be avoided. Enjoyment of food, fine wines and frolics is something to be relished at a civilised pace; this is aided by little formalities which make each of these things a miniature event in itself.

As many a wise mother has iterated: 'A little bit of what you fancy is good for you.'

Alcohol

Many are the delights of alcohol: golden Pimm's, ruby Bordeaux, silvery gins, emerald absinthe, the list goes on. The world of fine wines and liqueurs is a wonderful cornucopia, from the elegant bottles and artful labels to the curiously shaped glasses in which the drinks are served and, indeed, the intriguing ways that have been devised to serve them. We drink to celebrate and to commiserate, and there are few events in life for which some reason for a drink cannot be found. As Chapette Bette Davis once said:

> 'There comes a time in every woman's life when the only thing that helps is a glass of Champagne.'

Party Food and Drink

If you're the kind of gal who loves to throw a party, you might want to consider having a retro-themed bash of your own. Break out the Betty Crocker cookbook and try your hand at some genuine fifties appetisers like devilled eggs, cocktail weenies, shrimp puffs, stuffed pecans or silver-dollar hamburgers. In the States many people went mad for the 'Pu Pu Platter' – a selection of Oriental-inspired nibbles (meat and fish) which was a relative novelty at the time. No vintage party is complete without a host of classic cocktails and perhaps even a punchbowl!

Games

You've got your cocktails, your finger buffet and your music together – the icing on your party cake is a host of old-fashioned games to play! Pin the Tail on the Donkey is endless (and harmless) fun – you could even design and make the donkey and tail yourself. Charades is another game that's good for all and always good for a giggle. Twister is a retro party classic, but perhaps one for later in the night when everyone has settled in and a few glasses have been drunk. Whatever you choose, make an effort to include everyone who wants to play and don't try to force the fun if it's not happening – you can always have another cup of punch instead!

CHAPETTE

Congratulations!

You have reached the end of this nifty little guide. I sincerely hope it has been informative - or, if not, at least a bit of fun! The art of the Lady is one that takes a bit of work, but is truly worthwhile - a little bit of Chapette flair goes a long way! And remember, being a Chapette is about maintaining good form in all situations - which also includes having fun!

Yours sincerely,

Daisy Loveday

If you're interested in finding out more about our books, find us on Facebook at **Summersdale Publishers** and follow us on Twitter at **@Summersdale**.

www.summersdale.com